INTRODUCTION PROGRAMMING LANGUAGE FOR BEGINNERS

CODE LIKE A PRO

OLIVER LUCAS JR

Preface

Welcome to the exciting world of C programming! This book, "Introduction to C Programming language for Beginners: Code Like a Pro," is your guide to mastering this powerful and versatile language, even if you have no prior programming experience.

C might seem like a daunting language at first, with its reputation for being close to the hardware and requiring meticulous attention to detail. But don't worry! This book is designed to break down those barriers and make learning C an enjoyable and rewarding experience.

Why C?

In today's world of countless programming languages, why choose C? The answer lies in its enduring relevance and remarkable versatility. C is the foundation of modern computing, powering everything from operating systems and embedded systems to high-performance applications and game development. Learning C gives you a deep understanding of how software interacts with hardware, a foundation that will serve you well no matter what other languages you learn in the future.

What This Book Offers

This book takes a hands-on approach to learning C, guiding you through the fundamentals with clear explanations, practical examples, and engaging exercises. We'll start with the basics, like variables, data types, and operators, and gradually build up to more advanced topics like functions, arrays, pointers, strings, and file handling.

Who This Book Is For

This book is perfect for:

Absolute beginners with no prior programming experience.

Students learning C in a classroom setting.

Hobbyists who want to explore the world of programming.

Professionals from other fields who need to learn C for their work.

How to Use This Book

The chapters in this book are designed to be read sequentially, building upon the concepts introduced in previous chapters. Each chapter includes:

Clear explanations of key concepts with illustrative examples.

Practical code snippets that you can run and experiment with.

Engaging exercises to reinforce your learning and challenge you to apply your knowledge.

Your Journey Begins

As you embark on your C programming journey, remember that practice is key. Don't be afraid to experiment with the code, try out different approaches, and even make mistakes. The more you code, the more confident and proficient you'll become.

So, open your mind, fire up your compiler, and get ready to unlock the power of C! I hope this book empowers you to code like a pro and create amazing things with this timeless language.

Happy coding!

TABLE OF CONTENTS

Chapter 1

Diving into the World of C

1:1 Why C? The Power and Versatility of a Classic Language

Why C?

In today's world of countless programming languages, each vying for your attention with promises of ease and efficiency, why should you choose to learn C? It might seem like an old-fashioned choice, a relic from the early days of computing. But don't be fooled by its age! C remains a powerful and relevant language, and learning it can give you a significant edge in the world of programming.

Here's why:

Efficiency is King: C is renowned for its raw speed and efficiency. It's like the Formula 1 car of programming languages. When you need to squeeze every ounce of performance out of your hardware, C is often the best tool for the job. This is crucial for applications like game development, high-performance computing, and embedded systems where resources are limited.

Control Freak: C gives you unparalleled control over your computer's hardware and memory. You can manipulate bits and bytes directly, fine-tuning your code for optimal performance. This level of control is essential for system programming, where you need to interact directly with the operating system and hardware devices.

Universally Understood: C code is highly portable. Write your program once, and with minor tweaks, it can run on a wide variety of platforms, from powerful servers to tiny microcontrollers. This "write once, run anywhere" capability is a huge advantage in today's diverse computing landscape.

The Foundation of Modern Computing: Many modern programming languages, like C++, Java, and Python, borrow heavily from C. Learning C is like learning the alphabet of programming. It provides a solid foundation for understanding how software interacts with hardware, making it easier to learn other languages and grasp advanced programming concepts.

A Thriving Community: Despite its age, C has a large and active community of developers. This means you'll find plenty of resources, libraries, and support online if you ever get stuck. It's like joining a club of passionate enthusiasts who are always willing to help.

Learning C might require a bit more effort than some of the newer, more user-friendly languages. But the rewards are well worth it. With C, you'll gain a deep understanding of programming fundamentals, unlock the ability to write high-performance code, and open doors to a wide range of exciting career opportunities.

So, if you're serious about becoming a skilled and versatile programmer, C is an excellent place to start. Get ready to dive into the world of C and discover the power and flexibility of this classic language!

1.2 Setting Up Your Coding Environment (Compilers, IDEs)

Okay, you're fired up about C! Now, let's get your computer ready to write and run some code. Think of this as setting up your workshop – you need the right tools before you can start building.

1. The Compiler: Your Code Translator

C is a high-level language, meaning it's closer to human language than the ones and zeros your computer actually understands. That's where the **compiler** comes in. It acts like a translator, converting your human-readable C code into machine code that your computer can execute.

There are several popular C compilers available, each with its own strengths and quirks:

GCC (GNU Compiler Collection): This is a powerful and widely-used open-source compiler that works on various platforms (Linux, macOS, Windows). It's a solid choice for beginners and seasoned pros alike.

Clang: Another excellent open-source compiler known for its helpful error messages and faster compilation times. It's a popular alternative to GCC.

Microsoft Visual C++ Compiler: If you're using Windows, this compiler is integrated into Microsoft Visual Studio. It's a robust option, especially if you plan to develop Windows-specific applications.

2. The IDE: Your Coding Command Center

While you can write C code in any plain text editor (like Notepad), an **Integrated Development Environment (IDE)** makes your life much easier. Think of it as your coding command center. It provides a bunch of helpful features all in one place:

Code Editor: A specialized text editor with features like syntax highlighting (making your code more readable), auto-completion (suggesting code as you type), and code formatting.

Compiler Integration: IDEs usually have built-in support for compilers, allowing you to compile and run your code with a single click.

Debugger: This tool helps you find and fix errors in your code. It lets you step through your code line by line, inspect variables, and track down bugs.

Other Goodies: Many IDEs offer extra features like project management tools, version control integration, and built-in terminals.

Here are some popular IDEs for C programming:

Code::Blocks: A free, open-source, and cross-platform IDE that's great for beginners. It's lightweight and easy to use.

Visual Studio Code: A free and highly extensible code editor from Microsoft. With the right extensions, it becomes a powerful IDE for C development.

Eclipse CDT: A powerful and versatile open-source IDE that supports many programming languages, including C. It's a good choice for larger projects.

CLion: A commercial IDE from JetBrains specifically designed for C and C++ development. It offers advanced features like refactoring and code analysis.

3. Getting Started: A Step-by-Step Guide

The exact steps for setting up your environment depend on your operating system and the compiler/IDE you choose. But here's a general outline:

Choose a Compiler: Select a compiler based on your operating system and preferences.

Download and Install: Download the compiler and follow the installation instructions.

Choose an IDE (Optional but Recommended): Select an IDE that suits your needs and install it.

Configure the IDE: If you're using an IDE, you might need to configure it to work with your chosen compiler.

Write Your First Program: Create a simple C program (like the classic "Hello, World!" program) to test your setup.

Compile and Run: Use your compiler or IDE to compile and run your program.

Don't worry if this seems a bit daunting at first. Many online resources provide detailed instructions for setting up your C programming environment. Just search for "setting up C compiler on [your operating system]" or "C IDE for beginners."

Once you have your environment set up, you'll be ready to dive into the exciting world of C programming!

1.3 Your First C Program: Hello, World!

Alright, enough talk! Let's get our hands dirty and write some actual C code. It's tradition for programmers to start with a simple program that displays the message "Hello, World!" on the screen. It's like a rite of passage, a way of saying, "Hello, computer! I'm here to make you do amazing things!"

Here's the code:

C

```c
#include <stdio.h>

int main() {
```

```
    printf("Hello, World!\n");
    return 0;
}
```

Let's break down what's happening in this seemingly small but powerful piece of code:

`#include <stdio.h>`: This line is like bringing in a toolbox. It tells the compiler to include the `stdio.h` header file, which contains pre-written code for standard input and output operations (like displaying text on the screen). Think of it as giving you access to the tools you need to communicate with the computer.

`int main() { ... }`: This is the heart of your program, the `main` function. Every C program must have a `main` function. It's where the execution of your program begins. The curly braces `{ }` define the block of code that belongs to this function.

`printf("Hello, World!\n");`: This is the line that actually displays the message. The `printf` function is a powerful tool from the `stdio.h` library that allows you to print formatted text to the console. The text you want to print is enclosed in double quotes `""`. The `\n` is a special character that tells the computer to move to the next line after printing the message.

`return 0;`: This line signals that the program has executed successfully. It's like saying, "Mission accomplished!" to the operating system.

How to Run Your Code

1 Save the code: Save this code in a file named `hello.c` (or any name you like, but make sure it ends with the `.c` extension).

2 Compile the code: Use your compiler to translate this C code into machine code. If you're using an IDE, there's usually a button or menu option to compile the code. If you're using a command-line compiler like GCC, you might type something like `gcc hello.c -o hello` in your terminal.

3 Run the program: Execute the compiled program. In an IDE, there's usually a button to run the code. If you're using the command line, you might type `./hello` in your terminal.

If everything is set up correctly, you should see "Hello, World!" printed on your screen. Congratulations! You've just written and run your first C program. It might seem like a small step, but it's the first step on a journey that can lead you to create amazing things with code.

Chapter 2

Variables and Data Types: The Building Blocks of C

2.1 Understanding Variables: Storing Information in Your Programs

Imagine you're a chef in a bustling kitchen. You have ingredients scattered all over the counter, and you need to keep track of them while you're whipping up a culinary masterpiece. You wouldn't just leave them lying around without labels, would you? That's where containers come in handy. You store your flour in a flour jar, your sugar in a sugar bowl, and your spices in neatly labeled containers.

Variables in programming are like those containers in your kitchen. They are the essential building blocks for storing and managing information within your programs. Just like containers hold ingredients, variables hold data – numbers, letters, words, or even more complex information.

What Exactly is a Variable?

A variable is a named location in your computer's memory where you can store a value. Think of it as a box with a label. The label is the variable's name, and the contents of the box are the value it holds.

Why Are Variables Important?

Variables are crucial because they allow your programs to:

Remember Information: Without variables, your program would forget everything as soon as it moved on to the next line of code. Variables allow you to store data and access it later.

Manipulate Data: You can perform operations on the values stored in variables, such as adding, subtracting, comparing, or modifying them.

Make Your Code Reusable: By using variables, you can write code that works with different data without having to change the code itself.

Make Your Code Readable: Well-chosen variable names make your code easier to understand and maintain.

Declaring Variables in C

Before you can use a variable in C, you need to declare it. This tells the compiler:

The variable's name: This is the label you'll use to refer to the variable.

The variable's type: This specifies what kind of data the variable can hold (e.g., numbers, characters, etc.).

Here's the basic syntax for declaring a variable in C:

C

```
data_type variable_name;
```

For example, to declare a variable named age that can hold an integer (whole number), you would write:

C

```
int age;
```

Assigning Values to Variables

Once you've declared a variable, you can assign a value to it using the assignment operator (=):

C

```
age = 25;
```

This line of code stores the value 25 in the memory location associated with the variable age.

Using Variables

Once you've assigned a value to a variable, you can use it in your program. For example, you could print the value of the age variable using the printf function:

C

```
printf("Your age is %d\n", age);
```

This would print the following output:

```
Your age is 25
```

Choosing Meaningful Variable Names

When naming your variables, it's essential to choose names that are descriptive and meaningful. This makes your code easier to read and understand. For example, instead of using a generic name like `x`, you might use `age`, `score`, or `player_name`.

Variables: The Foundation of Dynamic Programs

Variables are the foundation of dynamic and flexible programs. They allow you to store, manipulate, and access data, making your code more powerful and adaptable. As you progress in your C programming journey, you'll discover how variables play a crucial role in building complex and exciting applications.

2.2   Exploring Data Types: Integers, Floats, and Characters

Now that you understand the concept of variables as containers for data, let's dive deeper into the different types of data that C can handle. Think of it like choosing the right container for your ingredients – you wouldn't store soup in a sieve or flour in a bottle!

C provides a variety of built-in data types, each designed to hold a specific kind of information. Here, we'll explore three fundamental data types: integers, floats, and characters.

1. Integers: The Whole Numbers

Integers are the workhorses of programming, representing whole numbers without any fractional parts. They can be positive, negative, or zero. Think of them as the counting numbers you learned in elementary school.

Here are some examples of integers:

```
10
```

```
-5
```

```
0
1000000
```

In C, you declare an integer variable using the `int` keyword:

C

```c
int age = 25;
int temperature = -10;
```

2. Floats: Riding the Waves of Decimals

Floats, short for "floating-point numbers," are used to represent numbers with fractional parts, like decimals. They are essential for handling values that require precision, such as monetary amounts, scientific measurements, or graphical coordinates.

Here are some examples of floats:

```
3.14
```

```
-2.5
```

```
0.001
```

```
1000.75
```

In C, you declare a float variable using the `float` keyword:

C

```c
float pi = 3.14159;
float account_balance = 1500.75;
```

3. Characters: Single Letters and Symbols

Characters represent individual letters, digits, punctuation marks, or other symbols. They are the building blocks for working with text and strings.

Here are some examples of characters:

`'A'`

`'b'`

`'?'`

`'5'` (Note that this is the character '5', not the number 5)

In C, you declare a character variable using the `char` keyword, and you enclose the character value in single quotes:

C

```c
char initial = 'J';
char grade = 'A';
```

Why Are Data Types Important?

Choosing the correct data type is crucial for several reasons:

Memory Efficiency: Different data types require different amounts of memory. Using the appropriate data type ensures that your program uses memory efficiently.

Accuracy: Using the wrong data type can lead to unexpected results or errors. For example, trying to store a decimal value in an integer variable will result in the loss of the fractional part.

Code Readability: Using appropriate data types makes your code more readable and easier to understand.

Data Types: The Right Tools for the Job

Just like a carpenter needs different tools for different tasks, a programmer needs different data types for different kinds of data. By understanding the characteristics of each data type, you can choose the right tool for the job and write efficient, accurate, and readable C code.

2.3 Constants and Literals: Fixed Values in Your Code

In the world of programming, not everything is meant to change. Sometimes you need values that remain fixed throughout your program's execution, like the mathematical constant pi (approximately 3.14159) or the speed of light. That's where constants and literals come into play.

Constants: The Unchanging Guardians

Constants are like variables with a special superpower: immutability. Once you assign a value to a constant, it cannot be altered during the program's execution. Think of them as the bedrock of your code, providing stability and predictability.

Why Use Constants?

Readability: Constants make your code more self-documenting. Instead of using a magic number like `3.14159` directly in your code, you can define a constant named `PI` which makes the code's purpose clearer.

Maintainability: If you need to change the value of a constant, you only need to update it in one place, rather than hunting down every instance of the value throughout your code.

Error Prevention: Constants prevent accidental modifications of critical values, reducing the risk of introducing bugs into your program.

Declaring Constants in C

You can declare a constant in C using the `const` keyword:

C

```
const float PI = 3.14159;
const int MAX_USERS = 100;
```

Once you've declared these constants, attempting to change their values will result in a compiler error.

Literals: The Face-Value Values

Literals are the actual values you use in your code, like the number `10`, the character `'A'`, or the string `"Hello"`. They are fixed values that are represented directly in your code.

Here are some examples of literals:

Integer Literals: `10`, `-5`, `0`, `1000`

Floating-Point Literals: `3.14`, `-2.5`, `0.001`

Character Literals: `'A'`, `'b'`, `'?'`

String Literals: `"Hello"`, `"C Programming"`, `"123"`

The Relationship Between Constants and Literals

You can think of literals as the raw materials for constants. When you declare a constant, you typically assign a literal to it:

C

```c
const int MAX_SCORE = 100;   // 100 is an integer
literal
```

Constants and Literals: Pillars of Stability

Constants and literals provide a foundation of stability and clarity in your C programs. They help you write code that is more readable, maintainable, and less prone to errors. By using constants for fixed values, you can make your code more expressive and easier to understand, both for yourself and for others who might read it in the future.

Chapter 3

Operators: Making Your Code Work

3.1 Arithmetic Operators: Adding, Subtracting, Multiplying, and More

Imagine you have a toolbox filled with tools, but you don't know how to use them. You might have a hammer, a screwdriver, and a saw, but without knowing how to wield them, they're just inert objects. Similarly, in programming, you have data (your raw materials), but you need operators to manipulate and transform that data into meaningful results.

Arithmetic operators are the fundamental tools in your C programming toolbox for performing mathematical calculations. They allow you to add, subtract, multiply, divide, and more. Think of them as the verbs in your code, the actions that make things happen.

Basic Arithmetic Operators

C provides a set of familiar arithmetic operators that you've likely encountered in your math classes:

Operator	Description	Example	Result
+	Addition	2 + 3	5
-	Subtraction	5 - 2	3
*	Multiplication	2 * 3	6

| / | Division | 6 / 2 | 3 |
| % | Modulus (remainder) | 7 % 3 | 1 |

Let's Break Down the Modulus Operator

The modulus operator (%) might be new to you. It gives you the remainder when one number is divided by another. For example, 7 % 3 equals 1 because when 7 is divided by 3, the remainder is 1.

Using Arithmetic Operators in C

You can use these operators with variables and literals to perform calculations in your C programs:

C

```
int x = 10;
int y = 5;
int sum = x + y;          // sum will be 15
int difference = x - y;   // difference will be 5
int product = x * y;      // product will be 50
int quotient = x / y;     // quotient will be 2
int remainder = x % y;    // remainder will be 0
```

Order of Operations: PEMDAS/BODMAS Rules!

Just like in mathematics, C follows a specific order of operations when evaluating expressions with multiple operators. The order is:

1 Parentheses: ()

2 Exponents: (not directly supported in C, but you can use the pow function from math.h)

3 Multiplication and Division: *, / (evaluated from left to right)

4 Addition and Subtraction: +, - (evaluated from left to right)

This order is often remembered by the acronyms PEMDAS (Parentheses, Exponents, Multiplication, Division, Addition, Subtraction) or BODMAS (Brackets, Order, Division, Multiplication, Addition, Subtraction).

Example:

C

```
int result = 5 + 3 * 2;   // result will be 11,
not 16
```

Arithmetic Operators: Your Mathematical Toolkit

Arithmetic operators are essential tools for performing calculations and manipulating numerical data in your C programs. By understanding their behavior and the order of operations, you can write code that produces accurate and predictable results. As you progress in your C programming journey, you'll find yourself using these operators extensively to solve a wide range of problems.

3.2 Relational Operators: Comparing Values for Decision-Making

Imagine you're at a crossroads, and you need to decide which path to take. You might ask yourself: "Is the left path shorter?" or "Is the right path safer?" These questions involve comparing different options to make a decision. In programming, relational operators allow your code to make similar decisions by comparing values.

Relational operators are the decision-makers of the C language. They compare two values and tell you whether a certain relationship holds true between them. The result of this comparison is always a boolean value – either true or false.

The Core Relational Operators

C provides six fundamental relational operators:

Operator	Description	Example	Result
==	Equal to	5 == 5	true
!=	Not equal to	5 != 3	true
>	Greater than	5 > 3	true
<	Less than	3 < 5	true
>=	Greater than or equal to	5 >= 5	true
<=	Less than or equal to	3 <= 5	true

Using Relational Operators in C

You can use relational operators with variables, literals, or expressions to form conditions:

C

```
int age = 20;
int voting_age = 18;
```

```
if (age >= voting_age) {
  printf("You are eligible to vote!\n");
} else {
  printf("You are not yet eligible to vote.\n");
}
```

In this example, the relational operator >= compares the value of the age variable to the voting_age constant. If age is greater than or equal to voting_age, the condition is true, and the code inside the first block (if) is executed. Otherwise, the condition is false, and the code inside the second block (else) is executed.

Relational Operators and Control Flow

Relational operators are often used in conjunction with control flow statements like if, else if, and else to create conditional logic in your programs. This allows your code to make decisions and execute different blocks of code based on the results of comparisons.

Example: Checking for Even or Odd

C

```
int number = 7;

if (number % 2 == 0) {
  printf("The number is even.\n");
} else {
  printf("The number is odd.\n");
}
```

In this example, the expression `number % 2 == 0` checks if the remainder when `number` is divided by 2 is equal to 0. If it is, the number is even; otherwise, it's odd.

Relational Operators: The Decision-Making Powerhouse

Relational operators provide the essential building blocks for decision-making in your C programs. By comparing values and evaluating conditions, you can create code that responds intelligently to different situations and inputs. As you delve deeper into C programming, you'll find that relational operators are indispensable for creating dynamic and interactive applications.

3.3 Logical Operators: Combining Conditions for Complex Logic

Imagine you're planning a weekend trip. You might have multiple conditions that need to be met for the trip to be a success: "The weather should be sunny" AND "I should have enough money" AND "My friends should be available." These conditions need to be combined to make a final decision. In programming, logical operators allow you to combine multiple conditions to create more complex logic.

Logical operators act like conjunctions in natural language. They connect individual conditions to form compound conditions. C provides three primary logical operators:

Operator	Description	Example	Result
`&&`	Logical AND (both conditions	`(age > 18) &&`	`true` only if both `age > 18` and

	must be true for the result to be true)	`(hasLicense)`	`hasLicense` are true
`` ` ``	`` ` ``	Logical OR (at least one condition must be true for the result to be true)	`` `(isWeekend) ``
`!`	Logical NOT (inverts the truth value of a condition)	`!(isRaining)`	`true` if `isRaining` is false, and `false` if `isRaining` is true

Using Logical Operators in C

You can use logical operators to combine relational expressions or other logical expressions:

C

```c
int age = 25;
bool hasLicense = true;

if ((age > 18) && hasLicense) {
  printf("You can drive!\n");
} else {
  printf("You cannot drive.\n");
}
```

In this example, the `&&` operator combines two conditions: `age > 18` and `hasLicense`. Both conditions must be true for the entire expression to be true and for the "You can drive!" message to be printed.

Example: Checking for a Valid Range

C

```c
int score = 75;

if (score >= 0 && score <= 100) {
  printf("Valid score.\n");
} else {
  printf("Invalid score.\n");
}
```

Here, the `&&` operator ensures that the `score` falls within a valid range (between 0 and 100).

Example: Checking for Multiple Conditions

C

```c
bool isWeekend = true;
bool isHoliday = false;

if (isWeekend || isHoliday) {
  printf("Enjoy your day off!\n");
} else {
  printf("Time to go to work.\n");
}
```

In this case, the `||` operator checks if either `isWeekend` or `isHoliday` is true. If at least one of them is true, the "Enjoy your day off!" message is printed.

Logical Operators: Building Complex Decision-Making

Logical operators are essential for creating complex decision-making logic in your C programs. By combining conditions, you can create code that responds to a wide range of scenarios and inputs. As you become more comfortable with C programming, you'll find that logical operators are indispensable for building sophisticated and interactive applications.

Chapter 4

Control Flow: Guiding Your Program's Execution

4.1 Conditional Statements: if, else if, else

Imagine you're a conductor leading an orchestra. You use hand gestures and cues to guide the musicians, telling them when to play louder, softer, faster, or slower. Similarly, in programming, you need a way to control the flow of execution, telling your program which lines of code to execute and when. That's where conditional statements come in.

Conditional statements are the traffic signals of your C programs. They allow you to create branches in your code, executing different blocks of code based on certain conditions. Think of them as the decision points in your program, where the flow of execution can take different paths.

The `if` Statement: The Basic Building Block

The `if` statement is the most fundamental conditional statement. It checks a condition, and if the condition is true, it executes a block of code.

C

```c
if (condition) {
  // Code to execute if the condition is true
}
```

Example: Checking for Age Eligibility

C

```c
int age = 20;

if (age >= 18) {
  printf("You are an adult.\n");
}
```

In this example, the `if` statement checks if the `age` variable is greater than or equal to 18. If it is, the message "You are an adult." is printed.

The `else` Statement: Providing an Alternative

The `else` statement provides an alternative path for execution when the `if` condition is false.

C

```c
if (condition) {
  // Code to execute if the condition is true
} else {
  // Code to execute if the condition is false
}
```

Example: Checking for a Passing Grade

C

```c
int score = 75;

if (score >= 60) {
```

```c
  printf("You passed!\n");
} else {
  printf("You failed.\n");
}
```

Here, if the `score` is greater than or equal to 60, "You passed!" is printed. Otherwise, "You failed." is printed.

The `else if` Statement: Handling Multiple Conditions

The `else if` statement allows you to check multiple conditions sequentially.

C

```c
if (condition1) {
  // Code to execute if condition1 is true
} else if (condition2) {
  // Code to execute if condition2 is true
} else {
  // Code to execute if none of the conditions
are true
}
```

Example: Assigning Letter Grades

C

```c
int score = 85;

if (score >= 90) {
  printf("Your grade is A.\n");
} else if (score >= 80) {
  printf("Your grade is B.\n");
```

```c
} else if (score >= 70) {
  printf("Your grade is C.\n");
} else {
  printf("Your grade is D or F.\n");
}
```

This code checks the `score` against multiple thresholds to determine the appropriate letter grade.

Conditional Statements: Guiding the Flow

Conditional statements are essential for controlling the flow of execution in your C programs. By using `if`, `else if`, and `else`, you can create code that responds intelligently to different situations and inputs. As you progress in your C programming journey, you'll find that conditional statements are crucial for building dynamic and interactive applications.

4.2 Loops: Repeating Code with for, while, and do-while

Imagine you're a factory worker on an assembly line. Your task is to repeat the same set of actions over and over again – pick up a part, attach it to the product, place the product on the conveyor belt. In programming, you often need to repeat a block of code multiple times. That's where loops come in handy.

Loops are the automation tools of your C programs. They allow you to execute a block of code repeatedly, either for a specific number of times or until a certain condition is met. Think of them as the tireless workers in your code, performing repetitive tasks efficiently and accurately.

The `for` Loop: Counting and Repeating

The `for` loop is ideal for situations where you know exactly how many times you want to repeat a block of code. It's like setting a timer for your code, telling it to run a specific number of iterations.

C

```
for (initialization; condition; update) {
  // Code to execute repeatedly
}
```

Initialization: This statement is executed only once at the beginning of the loop. It's typically used to initialize a counter variable.

Condition: This expression is evaluated before each iteration. If it's true, the loop continues; otherwise, the loop terminates.

Update: This statement is executed after each iteration. It's typically used to update the counter variable.

Example: Printing Numbers from 1 to 5

C

```
for (int i = 1; i <= 5; i++) {
  printf("%d ", i);
}
```

This loop will print the numbers from 1 to 5.

The `while` Loop: Repeating While a Condition Holds True

The `while` loop is like a conditional merry-go-round. It keeps executing a block of code as long as a certain condition remains true.

C

```c
while (condition) {
  // Code to execute repeatedly
}
```

Example: Reading Input Until a Specific Value is Entered

C

```c
int number;

printf("Enter a number (enter -1 to quit): ");
scanf("%d", &number);

while (number != -1) {
  printf("You entered: %d\n", number);
  printf("Enter a number (enter -1 to quit): ");
  scanf("%d", &number);
}
```

This loop continues to read input from the user until they enter -1.

The `do-while` Loop: Guaranteed to Run at Least Once

The `do-while` loop is similar to the `while` loop, but with one key difference: it guarantees that the block of code will execute at least once, even if the condition is initially false.

```c
do {
  // Code to execute repeatedly
} while (condition);
```

Example: Prompting the User for Input Until Valid Input is Provided

```c
int age;

do {
  printf("Enter your age (must be 18 or older): ");
  scanf("%d", &age);
} while (age < 18);
```

This loop will keep prompting the user for their age until they enter a value that is 18 or older.

Loops: The Workhorses of Repetition

Loops are essential tools for automating repetitive tasks in your C programs. By using `for`, `while`, and `do-while` loops, you can write efficient and concise code that handles a wide range of iterative scenarios. As you delve deeper into C programming, you'll find that loops are indispensable for tasks like processing data, generating patterns, and implementing algorithms.

4.3 Switch Statements: Handling Multiple Choices Efficiently

Imagine you're at a restaurant with a menu that has dozens of options. You could read through the entire menu from top to bottom, but that would be inefficient. Instead, you scan the menu, looking for specific categories or dishes that catch your eye. Similarly, in programming, when you have a variable that can take on many different values, and you need to perform different actions based on each value, a switch statement can be a more efficient and organized alternative to a long chain of `if-else if` statements.

Switch statements are like multi-way decision makers. They allow you to evaluate a variable or expression and execute different blocks of code based on its value. Think of them as a set of signposts in your code, directing the flow of execution to the appropriate path based on the value being evaluated.

The Structure of a Switch Statement

```c
C
switch (expression) {
  case value1:
    // Code to execute if expression == value1
    break;
  case value2:
    // Code to execute if expression == value2
    break;
  // ... more cases ...
  default:
    // Code to execute if none of the cases match
}
```

`switch (expression)`: This starts the switch statement and specifies the variable or expression you want to evaluate.

`case value1:`: Each `case` label represents a possible value for the expression.

`break;`: The `break` statement is crucial. It tells the program to exit the switch statement after executing the code for a matching case.

`default:`: The optional `default` case handles situations where none of the `case` values match the expression.

Example: Menu Selection

C

```c
int choice;
  \
printf("Menu:\n");
printf("1. Start a new game\n");
printf("2. Load a saved game\n");
printf("3. Exit\n");
printf("Enter your choice: ");
scanf("%d", &choice);

switch (choice) {
  case 1:
    printf("Starting a new game...\n");
    break;
  case 2:
    printf("Loading a saved game...\n");
    break;
  case 3:
    printf("Exiting...\n");
    break;
```

```
default:
    printf("Invalid choice!\n");
}
```

This code presents a menu to the user and uses a switch statement to handle their choice.

Why Use Switch Statements?

Clarity and Readability: Switch statements can be more concise and easier to read than a long series of `if-else if` statements, especially when dealing with many possible values.

Efficiency: In some cases, switch statements can be more efficient than `if-else if` chains because the compiler can optimize them for faster execution.

Organization: Switch statements provide a structured way to handle multiple choices, making your code more organized and maintainable.

Switch Statements: Efficient Multi-way Decision Making

Switch statements are valuable tools for handling multiple choices efficiently in your C programs. By evaluating a variable or expression and executing different code blocks based on its value, you can create clear, concise, and organized code that responds effectively to various situations. As you continue your C programming journey, you'll find that switch statements are particularly useful for tasks like menu handling, state machines, and parsing user input.

Chapter 5

Functions: Organizing Your Code for Reusability

5.1 What are Functions? Breaking Down Tasks into Modular Blocks

Imagine you're building a house. Would you try to construct the entire thing as one giant, monolithic structure? Probably not. Instead, you'd break down the project into smaller, more manageable modules – the foundation, the walls, the roof, the plumbing, the electrical system. Each module has a specific purpose and can be built and tested independently before being integrated into the whole.

Functions in programming are like those modular building blocks. They allow you to break down your code into smaller, self-contained units, each performing a specific task. Think of them as mini-programs within your main program, each with its own set of instructions.

Why Use Functions?

Organization: Functions help you organize your code by grouping related statements together. This makes your code easier to read, understand, and maintain.

Reusability: Once you've defined a function, you can call it multiple times from different parts of your program. This eliminates code duplication and saves you time and effort.

Modularity: Functions promote modularity, allowing you to break down complex tasks into smaller, more manageable pieces. This makes it easier to debug and test your code.

Abstraction: Functions hide the implementation details of a task, allowing you to focus on the higher-level logic of your program.

The Structure of a Function

C

```
return_type function_name(parameters) {
  // Code to be executed (function body)
    return value; // (if the function returns a
value)
}
```

return_type: This specifies the type of data the function returns (e.g., int, float, char, void if it doesn't return anything).

function_name: This is the name you give to your function, which you'll use to call it later.

parameters: These are optional inputs that you can pass to the function.

function body: This is the block of code that gets executed when the function is called.

return value: This is the optional value that the function returns to the caller.

Example: A Function to Calculate the Area of a Rectangle

C

```
int calculate_area(int length, int width) {
  int area = length * width;
  return area;
}
```

This function takes two integer parameters (`length` and `width`), calculates the area of a rectangle, and returns the result as an integer.

Calling a Function

To use a function, you need to call it by its name and provide any necessary arguments:

C

```c
int length = 5;
int width = 10;
int area = calculate_area(length, width);
printf("The area of the rectangle is: %d\n", area);
```

This code calls the `calculate_area` function, passing the values of `length` and `width` as arguments. The function calculates the area and returns the result, which is then stored in the `area` variable.

Functions: Building Blocks of Modular Code

Functions are essential tools for organizing, reusing, and modularizing your C code. By breaking down your program into smaller, self-contained functions, you can create code that is easier to read, understand, maintain, and debug. As you progress in your C programming journey, you'll find that functions are indispensable for building complex and sophisticated applications.

5.2 Defining and Calling Functions

Now that you understand the "why" of functions, let's dive into the "how." Defining a function is like creating a blueprint for a specific task. You give it a name, specify what kind of input it takes (if any), and outline the steps it needs to perform. Calling a function is like putting that blueprint into action, providing the necessary inputs and letting the function do its job.

Defining a Function: Creating the Blueprint

Here's the general syntax for defining a function in C:

C

```
return_type function_name(parameter_list) {
    // Function body (code to be executed)
    return value;  // (if the function returns a
value)
}
```

Let's break down each part:

`return_type`: This specifies the type of data the function returns. It can be any valid C data type (e.g., `int`, `float`, `char`) or `void` if the function doesn't return anything.

`function_name`: This is the name you give to your function. Choose a descriptive name that reflects the function's purpose.

`parameter_list`: This is a comma-separated list of input variables (parameters) that the function accepts. Each parameter has a data type and a name.

`function body`: This is the block of code enclosed in curly braces `{}` that defines the actions the function performs.

`return value`: If the function has a return type other than `void`, you use the `return` statement to send a value back to the caller.

Example: A Function to Greet the User

C

```c
void greet(char name[]) {
  printf("Hello, %s!\n", name);
}
```

This function, named `greet`, takes a string (`char name[]`) as input and prints a personalized greeting message. Since it doesn't return any value, its return type is `void`.

Calling a Function: Putting the Blueprint to Work

Once you've defined a function, you can call it from other parts of your program. To call a function, you simply use its name followed by parentheses `()` and provide any necessary arguments (values for the parameters).

C

```c
char user_name[] = "Alice";
greet(user_name);  // Calling the greet function
with the argument "Alice"
```

This code calls the `greet` function and passes the string "Alice" as an argument. The function then executes its code, printing "Hello, Alice!" to the console.

The Flow of Execution

When you call a function, the program's execution jumps to the function's definition, executes the code within the function body, and then returns to the point where the function was called.

Example: A Function to Calculate the Square of a Number

C

```c
int square(int number) {
    int result = number * number;
    return result;
}

int main() {
    int num = 5;
    int squared_num = square(num); // Calling the square function
    printf("The square of %d is %d\n", num, squared_num);
    return 0;
}
```

In this example, the main function calls the square function, passing the value 5 as an argument. The square function calculates 5 * 5 and returns the result (25), which is then stored in the squared_num variable.

Defining and Calling: The Dance of Functions

Defining and calling functions are two essential steps in creating modular and reusable code. By mastering these concepts, you can break down complex tasks into smaller, more manageable pieces, making your C programs more organized, efficient, and easier to understand.

5.3 Passing Arguments and Returning Values

Think of functions as specialized workers in your code's factory. To do their job effectively, they often need specific instructions or materials. These are the **arguments** you pass to a function. And once they've completed their task, they might have a result to deliver back to you – the **return value**.

Passing Arguments: Giving Functions What They Need

Arguments are the values you provide to a function when you call it. They act like the input ingredients for the function's recipe.

Here's how it works:

1 Function Definition: When you define a function, you specify the types and names of the parameters it expects to receive. These parameters act as placeholders for the actual values that will be passed later.

2 C

```c
int calculate_sum(int num1, int num2) {
    // num1 and num2 are parameters
    int sum = num1 + num2;
    return sum;
}
```

3

4

5 Function Call: When you call the function, you provide the actual values (arguments) for those parameters.

6 C

```
int result = calculate_sum(5, 3); // 5 and 3 are
arguments
```

7

In this example, the values 5 and 3 are passed as arguments to the `calculate_sum` function. Inside the function, `num1` takes the value 5, and `num2` takes the value 3.

Returning Values: Getting Results Back from Functions

A function can return a value back to the caller using the `return` statement. This is how the function delivers its output or result.

C

```
int calculate_sum(int num1, int num2) {
    int sum = num1 + num2;
    return sum; // Returning the calculated sum
}
```

In this case, the `calculate_sum` function returns the calculated `sum` value. When you call the function, you can store this returned value in a variable:

C

```
int result = calculate_sum(5, 3); // result will
store the returned value 8
```

Important Notes:

Data Types: The data types of the arguments must match the data types of the parameters in the function definition.

Number of Arguments: You must provide the correct number of arguments when calling a function.

Void Functions: If a function doesn't return a value, its return type is `void`, and you don't use a `return` statement (or you can use `return;` with no value).

Passing Arguments and Returning Values: The Communication Channels

Passing arguments and returning values are the primary ways functions communicate with the rest of your program. By understanding these mechanisms, you can create functions that perform specific tasks, receive the necessary inputs, and deliver the desired outputs, making your C programs more modular, reusable, and efficient.

Chapter 6

Arrays: Working with Collections of Data

6.1 Understanding Arrays: Storing Multiple Values of the Same Type

Imagine you need to store the names of all the students in a class. Would you create separate variables for each student? That would quickly become cumbersome and inefficient. Instead, you can use an array – a powerful data structure that allows you to store a collection of values of the same type under a single name.

Arrays are like organized containers with multiple compartments, each holding a value of the same type. Think of them as a row of mailboxes, each with its own address and holding a single letter or package.

Why Use Arrays?

Efficient Storage: Arrays provide a compact and efficient way to store multiple values of the same type.

Organized Access: Each element in an array has an index (a numerical position), allowing you to access individual values easily.

Iteration: Arrays work seamlessly with loops, making it easy to process and manipulate collections of data.

Data Structures: Arrays are the foundation for more complex data structures like matrices, tables, and lists.

Declaring an Array

To declare an array in C, you specify the data type of the elements, the array name, and the number of elements enclosed in square brackets []:

C

```
data_type array_name[number_of_elements];
```

Example: An Array to Store Student Grades

C

```
int grades[5]; // An array named "grades" that
can hold 5 integers
```

This creates an array named grades that can store 5 integer values.

Accessing Array Elements

You can access individual elements in an array using their index. The index starts from 0 for the first element and goes up to number_of_elements - 1 for the last element.

C

```
grades[0] = 85;    // Assigning 85 to the first
element

grades[1] = 92;    // Assigning 92 to the second
element

// ... and so on
```

Initializing an Array

You can initialize an array with values during declaration:

C

```c
int grades[5] = {85, 92, 78, 95, 88};
```

Iterating Through an Array

Loops are often used to iterate through the elements of an array:

C

```c
for (int i = 0; i < 5; i++) {

  printf("Grade %d: %d\n", i + 1, grades[i]);

}
```

This code will print each grade in the `grades` array.

Arrays: The Foundation for Collections

Arrays are essential tools for working with collections of data in your C programs. By understanding how to declare, access, initialize, and iterate through arrays, you can efficiently store, organize, and manipulate large amounts of data. As you progress in your C programming journey, you'll find that arrays are the foundation for many more complex data structures and algorithms.

6.2 Accessing Array Elements

You've created an array, this neatly organized container holding a collection of values. But how do you actually get to those values? That's where accessing array elements comes in. Think of it like having a set of numbered boxes – you need to know the box number (the index) to retrieve the item inside.

The Index: Your Key to the Array's Contents

In C, each element in an array is assigned a unique numerical address called an **index**. This index starts from 0 for the first element and increases sequentially for subsequent elements. So, the first element has an index of 0, the second element has an index of 1, and so on.

The Array Subscript Operator: []

To access a specific element in an array, you use the **array subscript operator** ([]). You place the index of the element you want to access within the square brackets after the array name.

C

```
array_name[index];
```

Example: Accessing Elements in a Student Grades Array

C

```
int grades[5] = {85, 92, 78, 95, 88};
```

```c
int first_grade = grades[0];    // Accessing the
first element (85)

int third_grade = grades[2];    // Accessing the
third element (78)
```

In this example, `grades[0]` refers to the first element in the `grades` array (which holds the value 85), and `grades[2]` refers to the third element (which holds the value 78).

Important Notes:

Zero-Based Indexing: Remember that array indices start from 0, not 1. This is a common convention in many programming languages.

Valid Indices: Always make sure that the index you use is within the valid range for the array. Trying to access an element with an index outside the array's bounds (e.g., `grades[5]` in the example above) can lead to unexpected behavior or program crashes.

Accessing Array Elements: Retrieving the Data You Need

Accessing array elements is fundamental to working with arrays effectively. By using the index and the array subscript operator, you can pinpoint and retrieve any individual value stored within an array. This allows you to process, manipulate, and utilize the data stored in your arrays to perform a wide range of tasks in your C programs.

6.3 Multidimensional Arrays

Imagine you're organizing a seating chart for a classroom. You wouldn't just list all the students' names in a single line; you'd arrange them in rows and columns to represent the physical layout of the desks. Similarly, in programming, when you need to store data in a grid-like or tabular format, you can use multidimensional arrays.

Multidimensional arrays are like arrays within arrays. They allow you to store data in multiple dimensions, creating structures like tables, matrices, or even multi-dimensional spaces. Think of them as a set of nested containers, where each container holds another set of containers, and so on.

Two-Dimensional Arrays: The Basics

The most common type of multidimensional array is the **two-dimensional array**. It's like a table with rows and columns, where each cell in the table holds a single value.

Declaring a Two-Dimensional Array

To declare a two-dimensional array, you specify the data type, the array name, and the number of rows and columns within square brackets:

C

```
data_type
array_name[number_of_rows][number_of_columns];
```

Example: A 2D Array to Store Student Scores

C

```
int scores[3][4]; // An array to store scores for 3 students with 4 scores each
```

This creates a two-dimensional array named scores with 3 rows (representing students) and 4 columns (representing different scores for each student).

Accessing Elements in a 2D Array

You can access individual elements in a 2D array using two indices: one for the row and one for the column.

C

```
scores[0][0] = 85;   // Assigning 85 to the first
student's first score

scores[1][2] = 92;   // Assigning 92 to the second
student's third score
```

Initializing a 2D Array

You can initialize a 2D array with values during declaration using nested curly braces:

C

```
int scores[3][4] = {

  {85, 92, 78, 90},

  {90, 87, 95, 82},

  {76, 84, 91, 88}

};
```

Iterating Through a 2D Array

Nested loops are often used to iterate through the elements of a 2D array:

C

```c
for (int i = 0; i < 3; i++) { // Loop through rows (students)

    for (int j = 0; j < 4; j++) { // Loop through columns (scores)

        printf("Student %d, Score %d: %d\n", i + 1, j + 1, scores[i][j]);

    }

}
```

Beyond Two Dimensions

You can create arrays with even more dimensions (3D, 4D, etc.) by adding more square brackets in the declaration. For example, a 3D array could be used to represent a cube or a voxel grid.

Multidimensional Arrays: Organizing Data in Multiple Dimensions

Multidimensional arrays are powerful tools for organizing and manipulating data in grid-like or tabular formats. By understanding how to declare, access, initialize, and iterate through multidimensional arrays, you can effectively represent and process complex data structures in your C programs.

Chapter 7

Pointers: A Key Concept in C

7.1 Introduction to Pointers: Memory Addresses and Variables

Imagine you're sending a letter to a friend. You wouldn't just write their name on the envelope; you'd need their full address to ensure the letter reaches the right destination. Similarly, in the world of computers, every piece of data you store in memory has a unique address. Pointers are C's way of working directly with these memory addresses, giving you a powerful tool for manipulating data and interacting with your computer's hardware.

Pointers are like special variables that hold memory addresses instead of regular values. Think of them as arrows pointing to specific locations in your computer's memory. By using pointers, you can directly access and manipulate the data stored at those locations.

Memory Addresses: Where Data Resides

Your computer's memory is like a vast city with billions of houses (memory locations). Each house has a unique address, and each house can store a piece of data (a number, a character, etc.). When you declare a variable in C, the computer assigns it a specific memory address where its value is stored.

Pointers: The Address Holders

A pointer is a variable that stores the memory address of another variable. It's like having a piece of paper with your friend's address written on it. You can use that address to find their house and even leave them a message.

Declaring a Pointer

To declare a pointer in C, you use the asterisk (*) symbol before the variable name:

C

```
data_type *pointer_name;
```

Example: Declaring an Integer Pointer

C

```
int *ptr; // Declares a pointer named "ptr" that can point to an integer
```

This creates a pointer named `ptr` that can store the address of an integer variable.

The Address-of Operator: &

To get the memory address of a variable, you use the **address-of operator** (&):

C

```
int num = 10;

ptr = &num; // Assigning the address of "num" to the pointer "ptr"
```

Now, the pointer `ptr` holds the memory address where the value of `num` (10) is stored.

The Dereference Operator: `*`

To access the value stored at the memory address held by a pointer, you use the **dereference operator** (`*`):

C

```
int value = *ptr; // Accessing the value at the
address pointed to by "ptr"
```

In this case, `value` will be assigned the value 10, which is the value stored at the memory address held by `ptr`.

Why Use Pointers?

Pointers might seem a bit abstract at first, but they offer several powerful capabilities:

Direct Memory Access: Pointers allow you to directly access and manipulate data in memory, which can be crucial for tasks like system programming and working with hardware.

Dynamic Memory Allocation: Pointers are essential for dynamically allocating memory during program execution, allowing you to create data structures that grow or shrink as needed.

Efficient Data Passing: Pointers enable you to pass large amounts of data between functions efficiently without copying the entire data.

Data Structures: Pointers are fundamental building blocks for creating complex data structures like linked lists and trees.

Pointers: The Gateway to Memory

Pointers provide a powerful way to work with memory addresses and manipulate data directly. By understanding how to declare, assign, and dereference pointers, you gain a deeper understanding of how C interacts with your computer's memory. As you progress in your C programming journey, you'll find that pointers are indispensable for many advanced programming techniques and data structures.

7.2 Pointer Arithmetic

You've learned that pointers hold memory addresses. But did you know you can perform arithmetic operations on these addresses? It's like having a map and being able to calculate distances or move between locations by adding or subtracting steps. This is pointer arithmetic – a powerful tool for navigating and manipulating data in memory.

Pointer Arithmetic: Moving Through Memory

Pointer arithmetic allows you to perform addition and subtraction operations on pointers. But unlike regular arithmetic, pointer arithmetic takes into account the size of the data type the pointer points to. This ensures that when you increment or decrement a pointer, it moves to the next or previous memory location that can hold that type of data.

Adding an Integer to a Pointer

When you add an integer to a pointer, the pointer moves forward in memory by that number of elements of the pointer's data type.

C

```
int numbers[5] = {10, 20, 30, 40, 50};
```

```c
int *ptr = &numbers[0]; // ptr points to the
first element
```

```c
ptr = ptr + 2; // ptr now points to the third
element (30)
```

In this example, adding 2 to `ptr` moves it forward by two `int`-sized memory locations, effectively making it point to the third element in the `numbers` array.

Subtracting an Integer from a Pointer

Similarly, subtracting an integer from a pointer moves it backward in memory.

C

```c
ptr = ptr - 1; // ptr now points to the second
element (20)
```

Pointer Difference

You can also subtract two pointers of the same type. This gives you the number of elements between those two pointers.

C

```c
int *ptr1 = &numbers[0];

int *ptr2 = &numbers[3];
```

```
int difference = ptr2 - ptr1; // difference will
be 3
```

Important Considerations:

Data Type Size: Pointer arithmetic is scaled by the size of the data type. For example, incrementing a pointer to `char` moves it by 1 byte, while incrementing a pointer to `int` (typically 4 bytes) moves it by 4 bytes.

Valid Memory: Be careful when performing pointer arithmetic to ensure that the resulting pointer still points to a valid memory location within your program's allocated space. Accessing memory outside your program's boundaries can lead to crashes or unpredictable behavior.

Why Use Pointer Arithmetic?

Pointer arithmetic is particularly useful for:

Traversing Arrays: You can efficiently move through the elements of an array using pointer arithmetic.

Dynamic Memory Allocation: Pointer arithmetic is essential for managing dynamically allocated memory blocks.

String Manipulation: Pointer arithmetic is often used for manipulating strings, which are essentially arrays of characters.

Pointer Arithmetic: Navigating Memory with Precision

Pointer arithmetic provides a powerful way to navigate and manipulate data in memory. By understanding how to add, subtract, and find differences between pointers, you gain finer control over your C programs and unlock the ability to work with data structures and algorithms more effectively.

7.3 Pointers and Arrays: A Powerful Partnership

Pointers and arrays in C have a close and intertwined relationship. In fact, they often work together seamlessly, providing efficient ways to access and manipulate data in memory. Understanding this connection can unlock a deeper level of control and flexibility in your C programs.

Arrays as Pointers (Almost)

In many contexts, an array name acts like a constant pointer to the first element of the array. This means that you can use pointer arithmetic to access array elements just as you would with regular pointers.

C

```c
int numbers[5] = {10, 20, 30, 40, 50};

int *ptr = numbers; // ptr now points to the first element of the array (numbers[0])


printf("%d\n", *ptr);    // Prints 10

printf("%d\n", *(ptr + 1));  // Prints 20 (accessing the second element)

printf("%d\n", *(ptr + 2));  // Prints 30 (accessing the third element)
```

In this example, ptr is assigned the address of the first element of the numbers array. Then, using pointer arithmetic (ptr + 1, ptr + 2), you can access subsequent elements in the array.

Array Indexing as Pointer Arithmetic

The array subscript notation (`numbers[i]`) is actually a shorthand for pointer arithmetic. When you write `numbers[2]`, it's equivalent to `*(numbers + 2)`. Both expressions access the third element of the array.

Benefits of Using Pointers with Arrays

Efficiency: Pointers can provide more efficient access to array elements, especially when dealing with large arrays or multidimensional arrays.

Flexibility: Pointers allow you to pass arrays to functions without copying the entire array, which can save memory and improve performance.

Dynamic Memory Allocation: Pointers are essential for working with dynamically allocated arrays, where the size of the array is determined during program execution.

Pointers to Arrays

You can also have pointers that point to entire arrays, not just individual elements. This is useful for working with multidimensional arrays or arrays of structures.

C

```c
int matrix[3][4]; // A 2D array

int (*ptr)[4] = matrix; // A pointer to an array
of 4 integers



// Accessing elements using the pointer
```

```c
printf("%d\n", ptr[0][0]);  // Accessing the first
element of the first row

printf("%d\n", ptr[1][2]);  // Accessing the third
element of the second row
```

Pointers and Arrays: A Synergistic Duo

The relationship between pointers and arrays in C is a powerful one. By understanding how array names can act as pointers and how pointer arithmetic can be used to access array elements, you gain a deeper understanding of C's memory management and unlock more efficient and flexible ways to work with collections of data.

Chapter 8

Strings: Manipulating Text

8.1 Character Arrays and Strings: The Heart of Text in C

While C doesn't have a dedicated "string" data type, it cleverly uses **character arrays** to represent strings. This might seem a bit indirect, but it gives you a lot of control over how text is stored and manipulated in your programs.

What's a Character Array?

Simply put, a character array is a container that holds a sequence of characters. Each character occupies one byte of memory, and they're stored one after another in contiguous memory locations.

C

```
char message[10]; // Declares a character array
named "message" that can hold up to 10 characters
```

Strings: Character Arrays with a Twist

What makes a character array a "string" in C is the presence of a special character called the **null character** ($\backslash 0$). This character acts as a marker, signaling the end of the string.

C

```
char greeting[] = "Hello";
```

In this example, the `greeting` array actually stores 6 characters: 'H', 'e', 'l', 'l', 'o', and the null character `\0` (automatically added by the compiler).

Why the Null Character?

The null character is crucial because it allows C functions to determine the length of a string and perform operations on it correctly. Without the null character, functions wouldn't know where the string ends in memory.

Key Differences and Similarities

Feature	Character Array	String (in C)
Data Type	`char[]`	`char[]` (with null terminator)
Storage	Contiguous memory locations	Contiguous memory locations
Accessing Elements	Using index and array subscript operator (`[]`)	Using index and array subscript operator (`[]`)
Null Terminator	Not required	Required (`\0`)
String Functions	Not directly applicable	Applicable (from `string.h`)

Working with Strings as Character Arrays

Since strings are essentially character arrays, you can use array operations to work with them:

Accessing individual characters: `char first_char = greeting[0];`

Modifying characters: `greeting[1] = 'a';` (changes "Hello" to "Hallo")

Iterating through characters:

C

```c
for (int i = 0; greeting[i] != '\0'; i++) {

  printf("%c ", greeting[i]);

}
```

Character Arrays and Strings: A Flexible Foundation

By understanding how strings are represented as character arrays in C, you gain a deeper understanding of how text is stored and manipulated in memory. This knowledge allows you to work with strings more effectively, utilizing both array operations and specialized string functions to perform a wide range of text-processing tasks in your C programs.

8.2 String Functions from the Standard Library: Your String Toolkit

C provides a powerful set of built-in functions specifically designed to make working with strings easier and more efficient. These functions, declared in the `string.h` header file, handle common string operations like copying, concatenating, comparing, and searching. Think of them as your specialized tools for string manipulation.

Here are some of the most frequently used string functions from the C standard library:

1. `strcpy(destination, source)`**: Copying Strings**

This function copies the `source` string, including the null character, into the `destination` string.

C

```c
char str1[20] = "Hello";

char str2[] = "World!";

strcpy(str1, str2); // str1 now contains "World!"
```

2. `strcat(destination, source)`**: Concatenating Strings**

This function appends the `source` string to the end of the `destination` string.

C

```c
char str1[20] = "Hello";

char str2[] = " World!";

strcat(str1, str2); // str1 now contains "Hello World!"
```

3. `strlen(string)`**: Finding String Length**

This function returns the length of the `string` (the number of characters before the null character).

C

```c
char message[] = "Hello";

int length = strlen(message); // length will be 5
```

4. strcmp(string1, string2): Comparing Strings

This function compares two strings lexicographically (like in a dictionary) and returns:

0 if the strings are identical.

A negative value if string1 comes before string2.

A positive value if string1 comes after string2.

C

```c
char str1[] = "apple";

char str2[] = "banana";

int result = strcmp(str1, str2); // result will
be negative
```

5. strstr(haystack, needle): Searching for Substrings

This function searches for the first occurrence of the needle string within the haystack string. If found, it returns a pointer to the first occurrence; otherwise, it returns NULL.

C

```c
char sentence[] = "This is a sentence.";
```

```c
char word[] = "sentence";

char *ptr = strstr(sentence, word); // ptr will
point to "sentence" within sentence[]
```

6. strchr(string, character): **Finding a Character**

This function locates the first occurrence of a specific character within the string. If found, it returns a pointer to that character; otherwise, it returns NULL.

C

```c
char str[] = "Hello";

char *ptr = strchr(str, 'l'); // ptr will point
to the first 'l' in "Hello"
```

7. strtok(string, delimiters): **Tokenizing Strings**

This function breaks a string into smaller "tokens" based on specified delimiters (e.g., spaces, commas). It's useful for parsing text.

C

```c
char sentence[] = "This is a sentence.";

char *token = strtok(sentence, " "); // token
will be "This"

token = strtok(NULL, " "); // token will be "is"

// ... and so on
```

String Functions: Enhancing String Manipulation

These are just a few of the many string functions available in the C standard library. By utilizing these functions, you can perform complex string operations with ease, making your C programs more efficient and capable of handling a wide range of text-processing tasks.

8.3 String Functions from the Standard Library: Your String Toolkit

C provides a powerful set of built-in functions specifically designed to make working with strings easier and more efficient. These functions, declared in the `string.h` header file, handle common string operations like copying, concatenating, comparing, and searching. Think of them as your specialized tools for string manipulation.

Here are some of the most frequently used string functions from the C standard library:

1. `strcpy(destination, source)`**: Copying Strings**

This function copies the `source` string, including the null character, into the `destination` string.

C

```
char str1[20] = "Hello";
```

```
char str2[] = "World!";

strcpy(str1, str2); // str1 now contains "World!"
```

2. strcat(destination, source): **Concatenating Strings**

This function appends the source string to the end of the destination string.

C

```
char str1[20] = "Hello";

char str2[] = " World!";

strcat(str1, str2); // str1 now contains "Hello World!"
```

3. strlen(string): **Finding String Length**

This function returns the length of the string (the number of characters before the null character).

C

```
char message[] = "Hello";

int length = strlen(message); // length will be 5
```

4. strcmp(string1, string2): **Comparing Strings**

This function compares two strings lexicographically (like in a dictionary) and returns:

0 if the strings are identical.

A negative value if `string1` comes before `string2`.

A positive value if `string1` comes after `string2`.

C

```c
char str1[] = "apple";

char str2[] = "banana";

int result = strcmp(str1, str2); // result will
be negative
```

5. `strstr(haystack, needle)`: **Searching for Substrings**

This function searches for the first occurrence of the `needle` string within the `haystack` string. If found, it returns a pointer to the first occurrence; otherwise, it returns NULL.

C

```c
char sentence[] = "This is a sentence.";

char word[] = "sentence";

char *ptr = strstr(sentence, word); // ptr will
point to "sentence" within sentence[]
```

6. `strchr(string, character)`: **Finding a Character**

This function locates the first occurrence of a specific `character` within the `string`. If found, it returns a pointer to that character; otherwise, it returns NULL.

C

```c
char str[] = "Hello";

char *ptr = strchr(str, 'l'); // ptr will point
to the first 'l' in "Hello"
```

7. strtok(string, delimiters): Tokenizing Strings

This function breaks a string into smaller "tokens" based on specified delimiters (e.g., spaces, commas). It's useful for parsing text.

C

```c
char sentence[] = "This is a sentence.";

char *token = strtok(sentence, " "); // token
will be "This"

token = strtok(NULL, " "); // token will be "is"

// ... and so on
```

String Functions: Enhancing String Manipulation

These are just a few of the many string functions available in the C standard library. By utilizing these functions, you can perform complex string operations with ease, making your C programs more efficient and capable of handling a wide range of text-processing tasks.

Chapter 9

Structures: Creating Custom Data Types

9.1 Defining Structures: Grouping Related Data

Imagine you're designing a database to store information about books. You need to store various pieces of data for each book, such as its title, author, year of publication, and genre. Instead of creating separate variables for each piece of information, you can use a structure – a powerful tool in C that allows you to group related data elements together under a single name.

Structures are like custom-made containers that can hold different types of data. Think of them as blueprints for creating complex variables that represent real-world entities, like books, employees, or students.

Why Use Structures?

Organization: Structures help you organize your data by grouping related information together. This makes your code more readable, maintainable, and easier to understand.

Modularity: Structures promote modularity by encapsulating data elements that belong together. This makes it easier to work with complex data and pass it between functions.

Code Reusability: Once you define a structure, you can create multiple variables of that structure type, each holding a different set of data.

Real-World Modeling: Structures allow you to model real-world entities and relationships in your code, making your programs more intuitive and reflective of the problem domain.

Defining a Structure

To define a structure in C, you use the `struct` keyword followed by the structure name and a set of curly braces `{}` containing the data members:

C

```c
struct structure_name {

    data_type member1;

    data_type member2;

    // ... more members ...

};
```

Example: A Structure to Represent a Book

C

```c
struct Book {

    char title[50];

    char author[50];

    int year;

    char genre[20];

};
```

This code defines a structure named `Book` with four members: `title`, `author`, `year`, and `genre`, each with its appropriate data type.

Creating Structure Variables

Once you've defined a structure, you can create variables of that structure type:

C

```
struct Book book1; // Creates a variable named
"book1" of type "struct Book"
```

Accessing Structure Members

You can access the individual members of a structure variable using the dot operator (`.`):

C

```
strcpy(book1.title, "The Lord of the Rings");

strcpy(book1.author, "J.R.R. Tolkien");

book1.year = 1954;

strcpy(book1.genre, "Fantasy");
```

Structures: Building Custom Data Types

Structures are powerful tools for creating custom data types that represent real-world entities or concepts. By grouping related data elements together, structures make your code more organized, modular, and easier to work with. As you progress in your C programming journey, you'll find that structures are essential for building complex data structures and modeling real-world scenarios in your programs.

9.2 Accessing Structure Members: Reaching into the Container

You've defined a structure, a custom container holding various pieces of related data. Now, how do you actually access and work with the individual data members within that structure? Think of it like having a toolbox with compartments – you need a way to open specific compartments to get to the tools inside.

The Dot Operator (.): Your Key to Structure Members

In C, the **dot operator** (.) is used to access the members of a structure variable. You place the structure variable name followed by a dot and then the member name to access that specific member.

C

```
structure_variable_name.member_name
```

Example: Accessing Members of a Book Structure

C

```
struct Book {

    char title[50];
```

```c
    char author[50];

    int year;

    char genre[20];
};


int main() {
    struct Book book1;

    // Assigning values to structure members
    strcpy(book1.title, "The Lord of the Rings");
    strcpy(book1.author, "J.R.R. Tolkien");
    book1.year = 1954;
    strcpy(book1.genre, "Fantasy");

    // Accessing and printing structure members
    printf("Title: %s\n", book1.title);
    printf("Author: %s\n", book1.author);
    printf("Year: %d\n", book1.year);
    printf("Genre: %s\n", book1.genre);
```

```c
    return 0;

}
```

In this example, `book1.title` accesses the `title` member of the `book1` structure variable, `book1.author` accesses the `author` member, and so on.

Using Structure Members in Expressions

You can use structure members just like regular variables in expressions:

C

```c
int current_year = 2024;

int age_of_book = current_year - book1.year;

    printf("The    book    is    %d    years    old.\n",
age_of_book);
```

Accessing Structure Members Through Pointers

If you have a pointer to a structure variable, you can access its members using the arrow operator (`->`):

C

```c
struct Book *bookPtr = &book1;

printf("Title: %s\n", bookPtr->title);
```

Accessing Structure Members: Working with the Data

Accessing structure members is fundamental to working with structures effectively. By using the dot operator (or the arrow operator with pointers), you can pinpoint and work with the individual data elements within a structure. This allows you to manipulate, process, and utilize the data stored in your structures to perform a wide range of tasks in your C programs.

9.3 Arrays of Structures: Managing Collections of Complex Data

Imagine you're managing a library catalog. You wouldn't just store information about one book; you'd need to store data for hundreds or even thousands of books. This is where arrays of structures come in handy. They allow you to create a collection of structure variables, each representing a different instance of the same type of entity, like a book, employee, or student.

Arrays of structures are like having a set of organized containers, each holding a complete set of related data. Think of it as a library shelf with multiple books, or a company database with records for each employee.

Why Use Arrays of Structures?

Managing Collections: Arrays of structures provide an efficient way to manage collections of complex data, where each element in the collection has multiple attributes.

Real-World Modeling: They allow you to model real-world scenarios where you have multiple instances of the same type of entity, like a list of students, an inventory of products, or a database of customers.

Organized Access: You can easily access and manipulate individual structures within the array using their index.

Code Reusability: You can define functions that operate on arrays of structures, making your code more modular and reusable.

Declaring an Array of Structures

To declare an array of structures, you simply combine the array declaration syntax with the structure type:

C

```
struct                         structure_name
array_name[number_of_elements];
```

Example: An Array of Book Structures

C

```
struct Book {

   char title[50];

   char author[50];

   int year;

   char genre[20];

};



struct Book library[100]; // An array to store
100 books
```

This code creates an array named `library` that can hold 100 `Book` structures.

Accessing Members of Structures in an Array

You can access the members of individual structures within the array using the array subscript operator (`[]`) and the dot operator (`.`):

C

```
strcpy(library[0].title, "The Lord of the Rings"); // Accessing the title of the first book

library[1].year = 1984; // Accessing the year of the second book
```

Iterating Through an Array of Structures

Loops are often used to iterate through the elements of an array of structures:

C

```
for (int i = 0; i < 100; i++) {

    printf("Book %d:\n", i + 1);

    printf("  Title: %s\n", library[i].title);

    printf("  Author: %s\n", library[i].author);

    // ... print other members ...

}
```

Arrays of Structures: Organizing Complex Data Collections

Arrays of structures are powerful tools for organizing and managing collections of complex data. By combining the capabilities of arrays and structures, you can efficiently represent and manipulate real-world scenarios involving multiple instances of entities with multiple attributes. As you progress in your C programming journey, you'll find that arrays of structures are essential for building sophisticated data structures and applications.

Chapter 10

File Handling: Reading and Writing Data

10.1 Opening and Closing Files: The Gateway to External Data

Imagine your computer's memory as a temporary workspace. You can create, manipulate, and use data within this workspace, but when you turn off your computer, everything disappears. To store data permanently or to access data that exists outside your program's memory, you need to work with files.

Files are like external storage units where you can save data persistently. They can reside on your hard drive, a USB drive, or even a remote server. In C, you can open files to read data from them, write data to them, or both.

Opening a File: Establishing a Connection

To work with a file in C, you first need to open it. This establishes a connection between your program and the file, allowing you to perform read or write operations.

C provides the `fopen()` function for opening files. It takes two arguments:

1 Filename: A string containing the name of the file you want to open (e.g., "mydata.txt").

2 Mode: A string specifying how you want to open the file (e.g., "r" for reading, "w" for writing, "a" for appending).

C

```
FILE *fptr; // Declare a file pointer
```

```
fptr  =  fopen("mydata.txt",  "r");  // Open
"mydata.txt" for reading
```

This code opens the file "mydata.txt" in read mode and associates it with the file pointer `fptr`.

File Pointers: Your File Handle

The `fopen()` function returns a **file pointer**, which is a special pointer that represents the opened file. You'll use this file pointer to perform operations on the file.

Checking for Errors

It's crucial to check if the file was opened successfully. If `fopen()` fails (e.g., the file doesn't exist), it returns a NULL pointer.

C

```
if (fptr == NULL) {

  printf("Error opening file!\n");

  // Handle the error (e.g., exit the program)

}
```

Closing a File: Releasing the Resource

When you're finished working with a file, it's essential to close it using the `fclose()` function. This releases the file handle and ensures that any buffered data is written to the file.

C

```
fclose(fptr);
```

Why Close Files?

Data Integrity: Closing a file ensures that all data is written correctly to the storage medium.

Resource Management: Closing files frees up system resources and prevents potential issues if you need to open the file again later.

Opening and Closing Files: The First Step in File Handling

Opening and closing files are the fundamental operations for working with external data in C. By understanding how to use `fopen()` and `fclose()`, you can establish connections to files, perform read and write operations, and ensure proper resource management.

10.2 Reading from and Writing to Files: The Data Exchange

Now that you know how to open and close files, let's explore the core of file handling: reading data from files and writing data to them. This is how your C programs can interact with the outside world, loading information, saving results, and persisting data beyond the program's execution.

Reading from a File: Input from the Outside

To read data from a file, you'll typically use the following functions:

fgetc(file_pointer): Reads a single character from the file.

fgets(string, size, file_pointer): Reads a line of text (up to a specified size) from the file and stores it in a string.

fscanf(file_pointer, format, ...): Reads formatted data (like numbers or strings) from the file, similar to scanf.

Example: Reading a Text File Line by Line

C

```c
#include <stdio.h>


int main() {

  FILE *fptr = fopen("mytext.txt", "r");

  char line[100];


  if (fptr == NULL) {

    printf("Error opening file!\n");

    return 1;

  }


  while (fgets(line, sizeof(line), fptr) != NULL)
{
```

```
    printf("%s", line);

  }



  fclose(fptr);

  return 0;

}
```

This code opens the file "mytext.txt" for reading, reads each line using `fgets`, and prints it to the console.

Writing to a File: Output to the World

To write data to a file, you'll typically use these functions:

`fputc(character, file_pointer)`: Writes a single `character` to the file.

`fputs(string, file_pointer)`: Writes a `string` to the file.

`fprintf(file_pointer, format, ...)`: Writes formatted data (like numbers or strings) to the file, similar to `printf`.

Example: Writing Data to a File

C

```
#include <stdio.h>


int main() {

  FILE *fptr = fopen("output.txt", "w");
```

```c
    if (fptr == NULL) {

        printf("Error opening file!\n");

        return 1;

    }


    fprintf(fptr, "This is some text.\n");

    fprintf(fptr, "The value of pi is approximately %.2f\n", 3.14159);


    fclose(fptr);

    return 0;

}
```

This code opens the file "output.txt" for writing (creating it if it doesn't exist), writes some text and a formatted number using `fprintf`, and then closes the file.

Important Notes:

Modes: Make sure you open the file in the correct mode ("r" for reading, "w" for writing, "a" for appending).

Error Handling: Always check for errors when opening files and performing read/write operations.

File Position: The file pointer keeps track of your current position within the file. You can use functions like `fseek()` to move the pointer to specific locations.

Reading and Writing: The Essence of File Handling

Reading from and writing to files are the core operations that allow your C programs to interact with external data. By mastering these techniques, you can load information, save results, and create applications that persist data beyond the program's execution.

10.3 Working with Different File Formats: Beyond Plain Text

So far, we've focused on working with plain text files. But the world of data is much richer than that! You have spreadsheets, images, audio files, databases, and many other formats that store information in specialized ways. While C doesn't have built-in functions for every file format imaginable, it provides the flexibility to work with various formats by understanding their structure and using appropriate techniques.

1. Text Files vs. Binary Files

Text Files: These files store data as human-readable characters, organized into lines. You can open them in a text editor and understand their contents. We've already seen how to work with text files using functions like `fgets`, `fputs`, `fscanf`, and `fprintf`.

Binary Files: These files store data in a raw, binary format that's not directly human-readable. They might contain numbers, characters, or even custom data structures, all represented as sequences of bytes.

2. Common File Formats

Here are a few examples of common file formats and how you might approach working with them in C:

CSV (Comma-Separated Values): These files store tabular data with values separated by commas. You can read CSV files by reading lines and then parsing each line to extract the individual values based on the comma delimiters. The `strtok()` function can be helpful for this.

Image Files (JPEG, PNG, GIF): Image files store pixel data in a compressed format. C doesn't have built-in image processing capabilities, but you can use external libraries like libjpeg, libpng, or libgif to decode and manipulate image data.

Audio Files (WAV, MP3): Audio files store sound wave data in various formats. Similar to images, you'll need external libraries to work with audio data in C. Libraries like libsndfile can help you read and write audio files.

Databases (SQLite): SQLite is a lightweight database engine that you can embed directly into your C applications. It provides functions for creating, querying, and modifying databases.

3. Strategies for Working with Different Formats

External Libraries: For many specialized formats, you'll need to use external libraries that provide functions for reading, writing, and manipulating data in those formats.

File Format Specifications: To work with a specific file format, you need to understand its structure and how the data is organized within the file. You can often find detailed specifications for file formats online.

Byte-Level Manipulation: For binary files, you might need to work with the data at the byte level using functions like `fread()` and `fwrite()`.

Example: Reading a CSV File

```c
C
#include <stdio.h>

#include <string.h>


int main() {

  FILE *fptr = fopen("data.csv", "r");

  char line[100];


  if (fptr == NULL) {

    printf("Error opening file!\n");

    return 1;

  }


  while (fgets(line, sizeof(line), fptr) != NULL) {

    char *token = strtok(line, ",");

    while (token != NULL) {
```

```c
        printf("%s ", token);

        token = strtok(NULL, ",");

    }

    printf("\n");

}


    fclose(fptr);

    return 0;

}
```

This code reads a CSV file line by line, uses `strtok()` to split each line into comma-separated values, and prints the values.

Working with Different File Formats: Expanding Your Data Horizons

While C doesn't have built-in support for every file format, it provides the tools and flexibility to work with a wide range of data formats. By understanding file structures, utilizing external libraries, and employing appropriate techniques, you can create C programs that interact with various types of data, expanding the possibilities for your applications.